In The Ink...

A Poetry Collection

M. A. Wells

The Wells Press

ISBN-13: 979-8-218-69830-0

Published: The Wells Press
Cover design by: M. A. Wells
Library of Congress Control Number: 2018675309
Printed in the United States of America

Contents

Preface

This collection was never intended to be a book. It began as scattered thoughts, late night whispers and words I could never say out loud. In The Ink... is a reflection of moments that shaped me, broke me and in some ways, saved me. These poems are fragments of love both given and withheld, things I carried in silence, and others still I tried to outrun. These works are not always tidy or gentle, but they are honest. Every page holds a part of myself I was once afraid to share. If you have ever loved someone too much, loved someone that didn't love you back, or felt as though you lost something you couldn't quite name; *this* is for you. Thank you for finding me *In The Ink...*

"A word after a word after a word is power."
MARGARET ATWOOD

For Zoey

In The Ink

In the ink
I tried to keep you here
Pressed between the lines
Folded into verses
To keep you safe from time

I wrote you down
To keep you close
Carefully
Line by line
But ink is colder
Then a hand to hold
And the letters
Don't quite shine

I carved your name
In whispered strokes
Soft like breath upon glass
Yet the pages do not echo back

Nor let the silence pass

I bled you into every verse
A love too vast to speak
But words dissolve
Like chalk in rain
And leave my paper weak

Still I write
For what else remains
When flesh and friend betray
At least within this ink-stained world
I can watch you
Fade away

Unspoken

Shadows dance
And whispers are broken
Lies a question
A solitary token
Was it the words that hurt?
Or something unspoken?
Within this enigma
Hearts and minds are broken

A symphony of silence
An orchestra of doubt
Echoing through corridors
Where secrets lie about
Each syllable spoken
Like an arrow in the dark
Piercing through the armor
Leaving a lasting mark

The tongue can wield a weapon

With words it can ignite
A blazing fire of emotions
Consuming day and night
But what of the unspoken?
The things left unsaid?
Do they hold a power?
A weight within our head?
They linger in the air
Like mist upon a lake
Ethereal and haunting
Their presence hard to shake

They carry hidden meanings
Within their silent core
The symphony of silence
Resounding evermore
The space between two hearts
Where connections cease
Yearning for understanding
Aching for release
Was it the words that hurt?
Or something undefined?
A web of emotions
Intricately entwined
Let us tread with caution
Choose our words with care

Honor the unspoken

The silence that we share

The Last Time

These bones that bind me
A framework of pain
Carved in memory
Shrouded by disdain

Struggling for balance
For a fragment of reign
But deeper I delve
Into this tempest of shame

The confines of certainty
The chains of my mind
You can't drown me out
No, I won't be confined
I'll rewrite my story
With verses all my mine
Not one word for you
No, not this time

Once inspired by your angelic face
Now you're just words I wish to erase
Bound by bone
Scribed in blood
This is the last time
I write the word "Love"
Lay it to rest
I shall retire
A final farewell
An ending entire

No Going Back

You told me you loved me
I remember that night
Laying on your roof
Bathed in starlight
I looked in your eyes
And fell deep inside
If only I'd known
The secrets they hide
But I can't go back
There's no turning back time

So here I am
With only a rhythm and rhyme

In verses I trace
The contours of your smile
In rhythms I linger
Lost in denial
As these pages fill

With my lovelorn plea
I yearn for silence
Just a moment to be free

To halt this ceaseless stream
This endless flow
To break the cycle
To finally let you go
Each lyric an echo
A bittersweet cry
A tale of devotion
That won't say "goodbye"
In every refrain
Your name softly weaves
Binding my soul
To the past it perceives

I'd Rather Be

In crowded streets
Or quiet little ways
Beneath the sun
Or the moon's
Cascading rays
Soaring through the stars
Or gliding through the sea
Oh, all the places
That I could be

In sunlit meadows
Or moonlit fields
Hand in hand with you
I silently yield
Your presence is a melody
Both pure and true
Of all the places I could be
I'd rather be with you

With your heart
As a sanctuary
Let the world spin
As it may
Even though it's all temporary
I'd be remiss if I didn't say
Of all the places I could be
I'd rather be with you

Lie To Me

Lie to me
If only for tonight
Say I'm the only one
You see
That your hands
Were made for mine
That your heart beats
Just for me
Say the words
And lie to me

Spin your words
Like a silver thread
Lay them softly
On my skin
Bring to life
What once was dead
Gasping
From within

Trace my name
In your whispered breath
Let it tremble
On your tongue
Hold me closely
Against your chest
Even when it comes undone
Say the words
And lie to me

When the morning
Steals the dark
When the truth
Comes into view
I'll hold these moments
Close enough
To almost
Make them true
I'll let your lips
Weave sweet deceit
And shape the dream
I cannot keep
Make each moment last
Your little lies
Erase parts of the past

Say the words

And lie to me

Face To Face

I've tried to put it into words
And tried again
But my words spill out
As string from a spool
No direction
No prose
Just dribble and drool

Face to face
I'm at a loss for words
But when pen touches paper
Where to start first?
With your kissable lips?
Or your dazzling eyes?
How do you hide your wings
Angel in disguise?

So soft and so kind
In the way that you care

I'm jealous of the wind
And how it plays with your hair
How the sun and it's light
Bathe your fair glowing skin
Or how the air of this world
Fills you from within
For when pen touches paper
Where do I begin?

Do I start at the part
Where your smile burns
Clear through my heart?
How you outshine any diamond
Any gem or star?
How no road, no path
No journeys too far
If you're at the end
I need only to start

Oh, the sound of your laugh
Makes me feel alive
And the tune of your voice
Stops the passing of time
I could go on all day
I could scribble on all night
But when we're face to face

The words

Don't come out right

Used To Be

We used to speak in midnight codes
In glances held and secrets sowed
You'd smile and I would read the lines
Between your words, between the times

We used to walk without a sound
Our fingers brushing, our heart's unbound
The world felt small, yet wild and free
Oh, how far we are from we used to be

Your laughter used to light the day
Now echoes where I've lost my way
I reach for you in memory's kiss
An angel I held, a life that I missed

We used to dream, or so I thought
Of places love could never be bought
But time teaches cruelly so you see
What's left behind, is what used to be

Now silence sits where you used to lay
And I forget the games we used to play
But some parts lament eternally
How far we are from we used to be

Winter Wind

The winter wind
It howls and moans
A lonely tune
That chills my bones
I'm isolated here
Alone
My spirits flown
My heart a stone

The snow outside
It falls and falls
A blanket of white
Envelops all
In my heart
There's naught but cold
A void within
A tale untold
The darkness comes
It takes it's hold

My mind a maze
That can't be strolled
I'm lost within
This wintry scape
A soul adrift
With no escape

The silence here
It echoes deep
A soundless void
That cannot speak
I'm lonely here
Just ghostly existence
A specter lost
In futile persistence

The winter night
It stretches long
The sweet abyss
Where I belong
Let the winter wind
Chill and blow
Let ice and snow
Obscure the show
But still, I hope

I yearn, I dream

For love and warmth

To be heard, to be seen

Wretched

I wear the name you gave to me
Stitched deep beneath my skin
Every thread a lie, each knot a plea
You've turned every smile into a sin

You drank from the wells I bled to fill
Then damned me for your thirst as it grew
You broke me just to test my will
Then laughed as the pieces clung to you

I've begged the stars to strike me blind
To never see what I became
This twisted thing you left behind
Still whispering your wretched name

You called it love, such a cruel charade
Of hollow vows and twisted games
You kissed the wounds your silence made
Then set my heart and house to flames

I've begged the stars to strike me blind
To never see what I became
This twisted thing you left behind
Still whispering your wretched name

You taught me love was learned in pain
That closeness came with cruel demands
I held my heart out in the rain
You watched it dissolve in your hands

I've begged the stars to strike me blind
To never see what I became
This twisted thing you left behind
Still whispering your wretched name

Pyres

In a war over words
Where verses take flight
Where emotions ignite
Like stars in the night
I'll spin a tale
Adorned with passion's true hue
Painting a picture with the line
You desire too

In a world ablaze
Where hearts beat as one
Where love's fire consumes
And the journeys begun
A love that burns
Forever fierce and true
I'd burn on the pyres
With you

Through realms of chaos

We find our release
In the fiery embrace
Our souls at peace
For passion's flame
Knows no retreat
It dances and flickers
As our two hearts meet

Through trials and tests
We'll forge our way
Together we conquer
Come what may
Through tempests and storms
Our spirits anew
I'd burn on the pyres
With you
For love is not timid
Nor bound by fear
It defies the odds
It draws us near

In the crucible of ardor
We find our strength
Bound together by a flame
That knows no length

Through darkest nights
Let us light the skies
With love's incandescent
Radiant ties
No matter the cost
No matter the view
Id burn on the pyres
With you

So let the world witness
Our fiery dance
Enraptured by passion's
Mesmerizing trance
For in each other's arms
We shall be reborn
Unleashing a love
Untamed and unworn

And when the pyres fade
When the embers grow dim
Our love eternal
Shall never be grim
In the annals of passion
Forever anew
I'd burn on the pyres

With you

Lightless

I can't find the light, in the dark
Can't be found
If you know not where you are
Trembling to the bone, a shell so thin
No more flickering in the wind
No more stars left to grow dim
Just the emptiness, I hold within

There's no more stars
Dancing in the skies
No more silhouetted dreams
Before my eyes
There's no more light
Left to find
Only me
My shadow and I

I can't find the light, to stir the spark
Can't read my words

When you're left in the dark
Hope and heartache, intertwined they may be
I'll embrace them both
For they shape what's Me
Every tear that I shed
Every scar that I bare
Carves a portrait of courage
A spirit that dares

There's no more stars
Dancing in the skies
No more silhouetted dreams
Before my eyes
There's no more light
Left to find
Only me
My shadow and I

The melody of memories
Both sweet and sore
Guides me through shadows
To the light once more
For even when the night
Is at it's prime
There's a symphony of hope
A rhythm in time

There's no more stars
Dancing in the skies
No more silhouetted dreams
Before my eyes
There's no more light
Left to find
Only me
My shadow and I

So I'll search for this light
Wherever it's concealed
In the beauty of moments
In love that's revealed
In the strength to move on
When I'm the one feeling frail
In the stories of tomorrow
Where dreams
Set sail

Muse

It's you who paints the colors
In my sunset and sunrise
My very first thought
When I open up my eyes
You're my moon at night
Gracing ethereal skies
There are only so many ways
So many words that I can find
To help you understand
Why it is I hide

You make my heart flutter
As if it were two love birds
You make it bend like a string
Singing a song without words
You make it play like a piano
And take flight without wings
When I look at you
I feel all of these things

I can't say it out loud
For I cannot find my voice
I'll let you draw the cards
I'll let fate make the choice

It's you who places the glimmer
On the surface of the sea
You're the song in the distance
Calling out for me
You're the name that I whisper
As I'm drifting off to sleep
You're the beat in my head
The tune of my melody
My muse

No Reply

I asked the shadows that haunt my room
The morning sun and the evening moon
I asked the stars if I'm to blame
If love's a fire or a dying flame?
The stars didn't fall, the sun didn't rise
The moon though full, gave no reply

I asked the rain as it kissed my face
To take your memory from this place
From the pages of things left unsaid
The empty space you left in my head
The fragile ghosts of another year
The echo of you, still lingers here
I begged the silence till my throat went dry
And still, no one can tell me
Why?

I asked myself beneath my breath
If love is life, then what it is death?
I asked the paged where my love once bled
The ink long dry, their meaning dead
I sought the flames that used to burn
But their warmth just won't return
I pleaded with time as it ticked by
How long must I keep wondering
Why?

For A Moment

It's all I can do to try and pretend
I'm not waiting for it all to end
If life's taught me anything
There's one thing I know
When it becomes dear
It's surely go
Like a glitter in the asphalt
Or the glint on fresh snow
It comes in waves and it's gone
Before you know

But for a moment I found you
And it was true till it wasn't
For a moment I had you
It was so beautiful, wasn't it?
For a moment I had you
It was quick and it was fast
Full of love that wouldn't last
When it fell apart

Theres no adhesive for a heart
All the pieces lay scattered around
I call your name
I silence the crowd
But for a moment
I had you

In the silence that follows I feel the void grow
My heart once full, holds only the echo
Of moments that linger
Like shadows they creep
Through the depths of my mind
They find me in sleep

But for a moment I had you
And it was true till it wasn't
For a moment I had you
It was so beautiful, wasn't it?
For a moment I had you
It was quick and it was fast
Full of love that wouldn't last
When it fell apart
Theres no adhesive for a heart
I lay the pieces at your feet
Every time that our eyes meet
From the moment

I had you

Words

Words linger long past the voice or breath
Heavy like the world
Perched upon your chest
They weigh like stone, they float as air
They build you up, they strip you bare
Words can light the dark
Words can fan the flame
Words can call you forth
Words can speak your name

They echo long after the silence falls
Etched in memories, carved in walls
Words beg forgiveness
Words start the fight
Words shape your dreams
Come each night
Words mend what's broken
Words break what is whole
Words can steal your peace

Words can soothe your soul

They twist like vines
They bend your will
Dull as a whisper
Sharp enough to kill
They carry truths too hard to bare
Or dress up lies with silken hair
They flower in hearts
Or leave them scarred
Word after word
They can hit
So hard

Audience Of One

Well, I've put it all down
On little scraps of paper
All my thoughts of you
That I save for later

It began at midnight
When we burned on the pyre
If my words had their way
I'd face death by desire

I sing only for you
My audience of one
It's been that way
From the moment I begun
I sing only for you
Beneath the trees
Hair pulled back

With a book on your knees

I sing only for you

So let these words dance
Upon a gentle breeze
And softly carry my love
Through whispering trees

In the pages of time
My stories just begun
So, I'll keep singing for you
My audience of one

Midnight Game

The stars above us twinkle and dance
As we lose ourselves in one another's trance
The silence of the night whispers our name
As two become one in this midnight game

I would murder the sun
To spend an endless night with you
And bask in the glow
Of a silver moon's hue
For in the darkness, we find
A different kind of light
One that illuminates our souls
Igniting passions might

The world around us fades away
As we hold each other never wanting to stray
The night sky is our endless canvas
Painted with love and a passion vast

I would murder the sun
To spend a night forever long
And hear the rhythm of
Your heart's archaic song
For in the darkness we find
A different kind of peace
One that makes all our worries
And our fears cease

Our love story written only in constellations
A tapestry woven by divine revelations
Each burning star is a witness to my devotion
Guiding us ever onward in celestial motion

I would murder the sun
Just to feel your embrace
And see the ecstasy in your eyes
That cannot be replaced
For in the darkness we find
Our true selves
And our love becomes a story
That forever tells

If My Words Had Their Way

In a world of whispered dreams
I reside
Yearning for a love
That echoes from inside
A tender longing
Deep within my core
For someone to love me
As I love them evermore

I've poured my love
Into words left unspoken
Sentences carefully crafted
With a heart laid broken
If my words had their way
They'd paint the skies
With colors of affection

Meant only for your eyes

Oh, how I wish
You'd feel the way I do
Embrace the possibility
Of me and you
A symphony of emotion
Both selfless and true
Begging you to see
The dream I pursue

I've laid my soul bare
In the verses and prose
Praying you'll accept
This passion that overflows
If my words had their way
They'd bridge the divide
Uniting two hearts
You and I
Side by side

But alas, the ache
Of unrequited love
A melancholy melody
Cooed by a lone dove

In these silent moments
I quietly yearn
For reciprocation
Another candle to burn
Yet still, I carry on
Even when it seems
That all hope is gone
Whispering prayers
In the nights that grow long
If my words had their way
They'd somehow reach your heart
And kindle a love
Written in song from the start

For love dear one
It is a journey to behold
It rises from the ashes
It makes us brave and bold
If my words had their way
They'd find their way to you
And start a new chapter
A story brand new

Until then
Ill keep safe the love I hold

Allow it to shape me
Each day as I grow old
For in the depths of my
Unrequited desires
I'll stay here alone
Tending to the faintest
Of fires

Foolish

Take this foolish heart
And this foolish man
You can hold it all
In the palm of your hands

The cracks and the scars
The dreams I outgrew
The words left unsaid
They're all yours too

All my broken hopes
Every silent ache
I'll give them to you
For love's gentle sake

I offer no mask
No well-rehearsed part
Just trembling hope
And a wide-open heart

With no promises left
Just the truth that I bare
If I fall apart
Let it be right here

So break me or keep me
Just know where I stand
Forever yours
If you'll take my hand

When your fingers close
And the silence stays
I'll wait for you
Through all of my days

So Easy

I feel the judgmental eyes
Collecting like knives
As they glare from the sides
My past actions they chide
How foolish of you
To think you're enough
Your tattered façade
Your edges too rough
From euphoria's embrace
To solitudes weight
Oh, how fickle the path of fate

If I cannot feel?
Then why do I ache?
If I lack the strength
How did I walk away?
It's so easy to think
It's so easy to say
How in the world

Did I end up this way?

The journey was harder
Than this hollow shell
The truth even harder
Still to tell
If we could converse
Have a conversation
We wouldn't be here
In this situation
You take one glance
And you think you know
You're all so eager
To cast your stones

I've come so far
From so far down
Can you tell me
Where rock bottoms found?
I know it well
I can give directions
I can point it out
Like my imperfections

If I cannot feel?
Then why do I ache?

If I lack the strength
How did I walk away?
It's so easy to think
It's so easy to say
How in the world
Did I end up this way?

The world is so harsh
When you're filled with doubt
It's colder still
When they won't hear you out
"You did it to yourself"
"You're a product of your choices"
I can already hear the sound
Of their voices
"Why don't you stop?"
"Have you even tried?"
Countless times
Stack them next to my lies
The stigma is real
It's tangent in the air
Where did they go?
Does anyone care?

If I cannot feel?
Then why do I ache?

If I lack the strength
How did I walk away?
It's so easy to think
It's so easy to say
How in the hell
Did I end up this way?

Death By Desire

In the heat of passions flame
I'm consumed
A willing sacrifice
Forever entombed
With fervent ardor
My heart beats anew
I'd burn in the fires
Face death by desire
For you

Like a moth to a flame
I'm irresistibly drawn
To the allure of your presence
To the song that's born
In your eyes a wildfire burns
I know it's true
Lost in this illusion
I'd surely burn for you

I'd brave the inferno
Unyielding and fierce
To feel the scorching heat
Of your touch my dear
For in your arms
I find both solace and truth
As I embrace the flames
Fanning my youth

Through the searing agony
I'd willingly go
To taste the ecstasy
Only you can bestow
For your flame knows no bounds
It burns so bright
Id surrender to you
Quietly, without fight

In the stirring of desire
We find our release
The melding of souls
A union of peace
In the tempestuous heat
Only passion rings true

I'd face death by desire

For just a moment with you

Blur

There are parts of me
That can't be found
Head in the clouds
Heart underground
They start as whispers
But they soon swell
Behind the mask I wear so well

Through shattered glass
Reflections blur
Where's time gone?
I can't be sure
I search for you
In eyes that gleam
Yet I only find you
In my dreams
In every shadow
Cast by night
I wait for you

In the waning light

My tangled thoughts
Is where you dwell
I hear your voice
As a distant bell

In the seconds
That our world's collide
I glimpse the love
I need to survive
I try to follow
I do my best
With this foolish thing
Within my chest

Through clouded veils
And dreams undone
You begin to fade
With the rising sun
And as dawn begins the day
I chase your ghost
As you slip away

Labyrinthine

In shadow's embrace
Where the light retreats
A labyrinth entwined
A real replete
Darkness beckons
Twisting paths unfold
A labyrinth of secrets
Stories untold

Lost am I
Amidst this dismal abyss
Navigating corridors
Of gloom, amiss
Echoes dance
In labyrinthine song
Whispered whispers
As I wander along

Oh, twisted paths

Obscured and entangled
A haunting maze
Where hopes are mangled
Through dim lit corridors
I strive to see
Guided solely
By my soul's own decree

No starry guide
No moonlit ray
Yet through the night
I shall press my way
With trembling steps
And a resolve unwaned
In the labyrinth's heart
May fate be ordained
The walls a tapestry
Of forgotten tears
Whisper tales of sorrow
Born of ancient fears
Every twist and turn
A test of resolve
As darkness swallows
Another puzzle to solve

The labyrinth's grip

It tightens still
Challenging my spirit
Testing my will
But in this web of darkness
I find my might
For within the shadows
Hides a guiding light

A flame
A flicker
A beacon unseen
Within my soul
Burns furious and serene
I rise above
The labyrinth's grasp
In every step
My courage
I clasp

Through chaos and confusion
I strive
To find the exit
Where hopes are alive
With every breath
I banish despair
This twisted maze

I shall conquer
I swear
For even in the darkness
Strength may be born
In every thorn
A rose is adorned
So fear not the labyrinth's
Eerie spell
For within its depths
Your spirit shall dwell

And when the final turn
Is taken with care
The journey at its end
My soul lay bare
The labyrinth's mysteries
I shall reveal
Transformed by the darkness
But still
I heal

Air

I've held out for something
Something soft and real
A trembling hand and a heart to heal
I'll peel back the layers
That I have long stitched tight
And present myself to you
In the fading light

A few words and a glance
To show that I care
I've left it all out there
It's all up in the air
There's no armor left
No clever disguise
Half hope, half fear
Before your naked eyes

So tell me gently
If you can see
The fractured parts
That make me, me
Will you turn away?
Will you venture near?
Will you understand
Why I hide in fear?

I'm not asking
For a promise in stone
Just a moment
That I don't feel alone
Take me as I am
Unsure and bare
And I'll take you
To breathe
As air

Modern Day Medusa

Your gaze, a captivating spell it weaves
Entangling my heart in a web of dreams
Within your eyes, ancient secrets reside
Mysteries of ages, tales of all time

Your lips, an alluring curve of temptation
Whispering verses, stirring the imagination
Each word you utter, a melody divine
Coursing through my veins, the sweetest of wines
In your presence I am lost
Mesmerized
A mere mortal entranced
By a Goddess, disguised
For your eyes are portals
To an immortal tale
Where passion and desire
Forever prevail

But Beware dear Medusa of modern day

For your beauty holds power, that may betray
Your charm, like a double-edged sword
It cleaves
Leaving in its wake
Shattered hearts and broken dreams

Yet still I am drawn to your ethereal grace
A radiance that echoes
Through both time and space
You possess beauty that defies mortality
Leaving even the Gods in awe struck envy
So let me bask in your enchanting embrace
Let your love be my eternal resting place
Though you turn me to stone with just a glance
I'd stay here forever, if given the chance

But beware dear Medusa of modern day
Of the hearts you ensnare
For your beauty a gift but a burden to bear
Through love's deadly path
You must tread with care
For those who approach
A fate they all share

For your eyes are portals
To an immortal tale

Where passion and desire
Forever prevail
Oh, dear Medusa of modern day
I'm helpless in your eyes and so I pray
Make me your statue, eternal here I'll stay
A monument to devotion
And a life thrown away

If I Could...

If I could hold you in my arms
I'd keep you safe from this world and its harms
I'd cherish you forevermore
And keep you close as my heart's armor

If I could hold you through the night
I'd keep you warm and hold you tight
I'd whisper love into your ear
And make certain that you felt no fear

If I could hold you through the pain
I'd take away your hurt and strain
I'd be your shelter from the storm
Keep you safe from the rain and warm

If I could hold you in my heart
I'd never let our love depart
I'd treasure every single day
And never let one slip away

If I could hold you in my life
I'd do all I could to make things right
I'd love you more with every breath
And never ever let you forget

If I could hold you just one time
I'd make it worth it, make you mine
Show you all the love I hold
And never let our love grow old

If I could hold you in our vows
I'd promise you to make them now
To love you always, through thick and thin
And to always stay in the moment we're in
For you're the one that makes me whole
The one that fills both my heart and soul
I'd dance with you under moonlit skies
Share laughter and love that never dies

If I could...

Simple Melody

Something so different, something so new
It's just as strange for me, as it is for you
I didn't have any plans, I had no design
I just picked up the strings
And started strumming in time

It's just a simple melody
To you it may not mean a thing
But from inside me, a symphony sings
It sings of a love that once flew on false wings
How getting to close to the sun
Is a dangerous thing
With every rise, every fall
It echoes in my veins
A serenade with poignant
Yet bittersweet strains
Each note, a brushstroke
Painting colors unseen
The orchestra of my heart

The canvas of my dreams

I've loved and I've lost
I've laughed and I've cried
These are the moments
That I felt alive
When I triumphed, when I failed
When I faltered and strived
It's all in the music
The melody can't hide
For these strings are my veins
Carrying these words from my heart
Just here in the moment
Playing my part

It's just a simple melody
To you it may not mean a thing
But from inside me, a symphony sings
I sat down in a chair
And picked up my guitar
And it floated through the air
Carried off from afar
Like a wisp in a breeze
Just a few simple bars
It's slow and it's quick
Like the passing of cars

It resonates in the hallows
Where longing resides
Carving pathways through darkness
Where love abides

Pages

Late in the night
When I'm cold and alone
Trapped in this house
Pretending to be a home
Do I pray to God?
Or just to the ceiling?
How will I ever shake this feeling?

Because we're the ones
That feel so lost
Who just want love
No matter the cost
We write these words
Despite the hurt
Drown ourselves in ink
Like we're dying of thirst

With each line we pen

We slowly unwind
The stories of our lives
The scars we can't hide
We find strength in each verse
In the tales we rehearse
As we navigate through life
For better or worse
We're not alone in this
We're bound by our art
Through the power of words
We can heal each other's heart
Just say you get it
Just say you feel
I couldn't give it to you
In a way more real

Theres nothing false or fake
Or even fabricated
In the way I breathe these words
Each one dedicated
Scripting the tale
Of my heart's silent fire
The pen finds it's way
Against my desire

We're the ones

That sit down with a paper and a pen
Make a promise to ourselves
To never love again
So let time be the author
Let fate be the sage
As I hold your memory close
And turn another page

If there's any love left in me
Just reach out and take it
For if I had no heart
Then no one could break it
I'll never say those words again
They belong to the ages
They'll stay here forever
On my unread pages
I'll keep those words safe
In the chambers of my heart
And let destiny decide when
Love is ready to restart

Hollow Man

I've run out of reasons
To keep up this charade
The mask has grown heavy
The smiles are all fake

Every word I've written
Now crumbles like a stone
A script abandoned
A story that's not my own

I've run out of reasons
To turn away from your eyes
To feign indifference
To believe my own lies

The walls I've built
Are fragile and thin
One more glance from you
And let the breaking begin

I've run out of reasons
To flee or retreat
The rhythm is lost
In my faltering feet

The echoes of maybe
Are washing away
The truth stays the same
At the end of the day

I've run out of reasons
But here I remain
Clutching at ghosts
And numbing the pain
Perhaps there's no answer
No solace left to find
Just a hollow man
And his love left behind

Caged

Here in my cage, just my shadow and I
A soul longs to wander, to break free and glide
Surrounded by iron, a captive it stays
Yearning for sunlight, just a moment in its rays

Outside the confines, the world dances with glee
Laughter and love, unburdened and free
A symphony of joy echoing from afar
While here in this cage, my own is left barred
I watch through the bars as they cherish their days
Embracing the warmth of life's vivid displays
Their smiles ignite like a resplendent flame
While I in my solitude yearn for the same

Each moment observed, my heart starts to ache
Oh, to be loved, to feel and partake
I marvel at the people, hand and hand they stroll
Their bond so profound as my cage takes its toll

Oh, how I envy the freedom they possess
Each stolen kiss, a tormenting caress
Yet I'm left alone, a silent captive soul
My spirit crushed, my heart paying the toll

In this tapestry of life, I'm a thread yet unweaved
Unable to join in, my spirit bereaved
A mosaic of feelings, working only in blues
I crave liberation, to chase what I choose
The birds overhead sing their songs in delight
Their wings reach for skies, embracing the light
I dream of ascending like them to the air
To taste a cloud's kiss and to find solace there

Oh, to be free, to soar amongst the skies
To taste the sweet essence of love's paradise
But destiny, cruel fate, has bound me up tight
In this desolate cage, devoid of all light

In the depths of despair, I search for a glimmer
A flicker of hope, a reason to shimmer
But the walls of my cage, they close- in so tight
Suffocating dreams and extinguishing the light

Yet deep in my heart, a fire still burns
A sliver of hope, a fragile soul that learns
To break through these barriers, to find my own way
And reclaim my life, no longer thrown away

So let me be patient, let me find my voice
Within this cage, I'll discover the power of choice
For life's truest freedom, hides not behind walls
But in how we rise, when all else tells us to fall

And when the day dawns, when these shackles release
Ill emerge from the darkness, finally unleashed
No longer a captive, no longer in pain
I'll dance with the wind and be whole once again
I'll cherish the fragments of joy that I see
Through the bars of my cage, let my spirit be free
For though love eludes me and freedom seems far
I'll find solace within, beneath hope's distant star

The Reason

I watch you dance and I wonder why?
In the soft glow of a flickering streetlight
I watch you dance
What a pleasure
What a sight
Your every move
A dark melody
The longing stirred
And I whispered a plea

From afar
I trace your elegant lines
Enchanted by the way
Your aura shines
With every step
I hear a sonnet in the air
With every twirl
I can't help but stare

Oh, how I wish
To be the reason why
You spin and whirl
Beneath this starry sky
To be the song in your sway
The tune of your melody
To be the reason you dance
Only for me

To hold your hand
And share in the dance
To be in our own world
Our own romance

Checked Out

In the library of my heart
A book left unread
Pages left unturned
And words left unsaid
Each chapter a glimpse
Of a transfixed soul
Whispers and secrets
A paper heart to hold
In your eyes I see a window
That holds enchanted lands
Where dreams and desires
Interlace as familiar strands

Your smile is the verse
That calls out
My hidden muse
Your gentle ink
That scrawls upon my skin
Words of lust and passion

Of desire held within
So let me be the reader
The reader of your soul
Within ink and passion
Let our story unfold

Shattered Crown

In the echoes of silence
A monarch's lament
Threads of dreams
In shadows are spent
Yet from the ashes
Resilience shall rise
Mending the fractures
Turning the tides

You've stolen the key to my kingdom
Taken the bells so no one can ring them
You've locked all the doors
And barred the gate
But in the end
All you've sealed is your fate
When thy kingdom come
And my will is done
Who will it be?
Who has fought and won?

With borders crossed
And the lines now blurred
In this fallen kingdom
This wreckage of words
Don't be a fool
Don't be absurd
I'm taking it back
I'm storming the keep
You reap what you sow
And you sow what you reap
You may have the key
Just know that in time
I'm taking it back
It's rightfully mine

Love Lay Dying

It didn't end in thunderclaps
No storm torn skies
No shattered glass
It faded like an ancient vow
Forgotten, scattered to the wind
Somehow

No battles waged
No final plea
Just the silence
Where your voice should be
A colder bed
A hollow glance
And aging legs
That once knew how to dance
We used to bloom
In words and flame
But now it seems
I can barely speak your name

The laughter dried
The warmth withdrew
Even the "goodbye" seems
Long overdue
Love did not fall
With a sword in hand
Nor burn like wildfire
Razing the land
It starved beneath
A quiet sun
Unseen, unloved, undone

Yet still
I'll hold the ashes
Near and dear
Like some old song
That we used to hear
Not mourning out loud
Just humming low
This is how it feels
This is how I know
The death of love
Is soft and slow

Deny The Gates

Heaven's glow and celestial gleam
Fade before you, my radiant dream
For the angels may beckon
From high above
Yet, I'd descend for just one lifetime of love
Among the cosmos
Out where stardust collides
Id forever choose our dance
Over the ethereal tides

I'd trade all my time in heaven
For just this life with you
For heavens treasures, the celestial above
Dim beside you and your earthly love
I'd trade the endless, for one fleeting breath
I'd forsake eternity and plead with life and death

In a tapestry from, forever spun
I'd unravel the threads, save for the one
I'd barter eternity, trade time and space
For one earthly lifetime
With you and your grace
For the angels may envy
And seraphim my sigh
Yet even the heavens seem dark
Compared to your eyes

Your Name

Your name hits softly and quietly
It dissolves on my tongue
You pulse through my veins
Until my heart begins to flood
I carry you in the pauses
In the breaths I forget to take
In the spaces between what I mean
And what I say

I feel you deep in the silent weight of
My restraint
In the touch my trembling hands
Dare not to make
In the caress, the kiss, the chance
I'll never take
It's electrical, chemical
It's hardwired in our brains

A force I can't deny

It never bends, it never breaks
It sings beneath my skin
With every move that I make
I play the distant role
I wear composure as a mask
But I'd shed it all for you
If only you'd ask

So, I'll hold you in the quiet
Where the aching stays contained
Where longing learns obedience
And desire dawns its chains
Still my heart knows the truth
My lips will never say

Take Me Under

I can't meet your eyes
For fear I'll fall inside
A single glance
Just one mistake
That's all it will take
And I'll be drowning
Lost to the lake of you

Take me under
Pull me in
With hearts at war
And bodies that sin
Minds that lie
Devils in disguise
I'll show you
I'll tear the veil from your eyes

When the sin subsides

When the tide recedes
Will you remain?
Or leave me to bleed?
For hearts like ours
Aren't meant to heal
Only to shatter
And only to feel
When dawn arrives
With the sun's decree
Will you still crave
The darkness in me?
Will you love the rubble?
The tattered remains?
Or will you curse the night
You unshackled my chains

Take me under
Pull me in
With hearts at war
And bodies that sin
Minds that lie
Devils in disguise
I'll show you
I'll tear the veil from your eyes

Your eyes hold secrets

I can't resist

Your venom laced

In every kiss

The moonlight glows

A pale blue hue

Revealing me

Revealing you

No mask

No lies

No just flesh and bone

For here in the dark
I'm yours alone

Take me under

Pull me in

With hearts at war

And bodies that sin

Minds that lie

Devils in disguise

I'll show you

I'll tear the veil from your eyes

Ink

In the depths of reminiscence
I ponder and recall
A time when innocence reigned
Unburdened by it all
When my soul wandered freely
Untethered and unbound
Before the weight of expectations
Brought me to the ground

Oh, how I wonder
If those days were truly sublime
Before I delved into the realm
Of rhythm and rhyme
When my heart beat in silence
Untouched by your allure
Before I unveiled my inner thoughts
Vulnerable and pure

As I traverse this path

Strewn with doubt and fear
I find solace in the melodies
That flow from my tears
For within the ink-stained pages
A piece of me resides
A testament to love and longing
I'll forever hide

Though my words may echo loudly
Heard by countless ears
There's a part of me that yearns for
Those simpler years
When love was a secret
Hidden deep within my core
Before the world embraced the verses
That I have long adored
In the quiet of the night
Where shadows dance and sway
Silhouettes of forgotten dreams
They gently come to play
Breathing life into my musings
Igniting passion's fire
The melody unfurls
Laced with my desire

As I traverse this path

Strewn with doubt and fear
I find solace in the melodies
That flow from my tears
For within the ink-stained pages
A piece of me resides
A testament to love and longing
I'll forever hide

Through valleys of uncertainty
I wander far and wide
Seeking solace in the words
That in my heart resides
With every stroke of the pen
My mind begins to soar
Unveiling tales of passion
And the secrets I once bore

A cadence in the silence
A call for inner peace
In the melodies of longing
My heart finds its release
The ink spills like a river
Flowing from my veins
Transcribing my emotions
As they fall as blackened rain

As the ink embraces paper
A dance
Forever entwined
The stories of my journey
Whispered by my heart and mind
Each syllable a brushstroke
Creating worlds yet unknown
Where love's eternal seed
In sacred fields are sown

Legacy's Echo

In the darkrooms of life
We develop our story
A careful collage
Moments in love and glory
As we journey through time
We touch many hearts
Leaving footprints behind
That our lives impart

May I be a beacon
A steady guiding light
Bringing moments of joy
And dispelling the night
May my presence be a whisper
Deep within your souls
A gentle breeze that stirs
Somehow letting them know
Let my laughter echo
In their memory's embrace

A symphony of mirth
A smile on their face
May my tears be the rain
That nourishes their growth
Watering the seeds of hope and compassion
Inspiring both

For in the moments we share
Memories take root
In the depths of our hearts
Like seeds
They shoot
The echoes of laughter
The warmth of a familiar embrace
Shall forever reside
Leaving a lasting trace
And when sadness befalls
As it oftentimes will
May my memory linger
May your cup be filled
A shoulder to lean on
A hand to hold tight
Together we'll weather
The darkest of nights

Above all

Let love be the legacy I leave
A song that endures
And hearts shall perceive
For love is the essence
The language of the soul
Connecting us together
Making us whole

So let me be the vessel
That carries love's flame
Igniting hearts
With passion's unflinching aim
May the lives I've touched
Be blessed and inspired
With moments and memories
And happiness acquired

As the tapestry of my life
Nears its bitter end
May the threads that I've woven
Continue to mend
A legacy of love
An echo in eternity
In the hearts of all those
Who shared this journey

I leave you my passion
My words and my prose
For when the time comes
When my life's at its close
When the curtains fall
And the lights go out
I'll leave you without
A shadow of a doubt
That though I leave you
I loved you throughout

For this I pledge
I promise
I swear
When you close your eyes
I
Will
Aways
Be
There...

About The Author

M. A. Wells

My name is M. A. Wells. I was born out of Louisville, Kentucky. I come from a humble but troubled background. As with us all, that background has shaped a significant part of who I am today. For much of my life I struggled with addiction and depression. As a youth, writing became the only place I could be honest. It gave me a place to wrestle with pain, find a little clarity amongst the chaos and speak words I often could not say out loud.

In The Ink... is my first published collection. These poems come from the parts of me I've kept hidden, some were written during the most defining and darkest times of my life. These words serve as proof that I am still here, still trying, still learning how to turn pain into something worth holding onto.

Contact

E-Mail: AuthorMAWells@gmail.com

and on Instagram:

@AuthorMAWells

www.ingramcontent.com/pod-product-compliance
Lightning Source LLC
LaVergne TN
LVHW010626100826
845148LV00014B/3122

* 9 7 9 8 2 1 8 6 9 8 3 0 0 *